# VIDEO MARKETI NG

## Using video content to increase brand recognition and How to Develop a High-Level Product That Works and All the Information You Need to Grow Your Business and Boost Sales

### RICHARD N. WILLIAMS

# TABLE OF CONTENTS

# INTRODUCT ION

In the clamoring roads of a cutting edge city, Rachel wound up in charge of a striving startup. She set out on a journey that would change her fortunes and revolutionize how the world perceived her brand because she was determined to give her business new life.

Visionary entrepreneur Rachel recognized the digital age's potential for video marketing. With a strong soul, she submerged herself in understanding the complexities of saddling the force of video content for brand mindfulness. No fantasies here — simply a persevering lady dealing with the difficulties of the business world directly.

Her most memorable advancement came when she coincidentally found a little group of inventive personalities who shared her enthusiasm. Together, they dug into the specialty of narrating through recordings, making stories that went past the customary. They were aware that authenticity was the currency of connection in the cluttered digital landscape.

The group began by incorporating the brand's story into short, powerful, and popular videos. Each edge was a cautiously organized piece of the brand's quintessence, conveying items as well as the qualities and goals behind them. These weren't simple commercials; they were convincing stories that connected with watchers on a more profound level.

Their most memorable video, an in the background look into the creation of their leader item, earned consideration past assumptions. Individuals weren't simply purchasing an item; they were putting resources into an excursion. The video filled in as an impetus for brand steadfastness, producing a close to home association that rose above the value-based.

Unflinching by the underlying difficulties, Rachel and her group kept on developing. They investigated intelligent recordings, permitting watchers to be essential for the brand insight. Through surveys and tests implanted in the substance, they changed latent watchers into dynamic members, encouraging a feeling of inclusivity.

The strength of their soul was tried when a pandemic cleared across the globe. Organizations covered, economies faltered, however Rachel saw an open door in the midst of the mayhem. Perceiving the flood in web-based exercises, she turned her technique, making video content that reverberated with the ongoing reality. From endearing accounts of representatives adjusting to remote work to displaying the organization's obligation to local area government assistance, the recordings turned into an encouraging sign in questionable times.

As the brand's web-based presence prospered, so did the measurements. Rachel carefully followed commitment, change rates, and client criticism. The information turned into her compass, directing the group to constantly refine their methodology. They found the force of video tributes, transforming fulfilled clients into brand advocates. Legitimate voices resounded definitely more than any promoting slogan.

Embracing development, they wandered into live recordings, associating with their crowd continuously. Rachel became the face of these meetings, giving advice, answering questions, and making the brand more relatable to people. The live organization added an individual touch, changing the one sided discussion into a unique exchange.

The effect undulated across virtual entertainment stages, with watchers enthusiastically expecting every video discharge. Rachel's excursion from a striving business visionary to a trailblazer in video showcasing was a demonstration of the groundbreaking capability of strength and development. Her story propelled others to embrace change, to see difficulties not as road obstructions but rather as any open doors for development.

As the brand kept on prospering, Rachel's obligation to social obligation turned into a foundation of their video content. They started crusades resolving major problems, utilizing their foundation to bring issues to light and drive positive change. The recordings turned into a power for good, displaying that a brand's impact could stretch out past overall revenues.

In meeting rooms and showcasing classes, Rachel turned into a sought-after speaker, sharing the illustrations gained from her extraordinary excursion. She underscored the significance of validness, development, and a versatile soul in exploring the consistently developing scene of video showcasing. Eventually, Rachel's story wasn't a fantasy, yet an unmistakable illustration of what happens when enthusiasm meets development, and strength turns into the main thrust. Video promoting, when a strange domain for her striving startup, turned into the foundation of their prosperity. In a world immersed with content, Rachel demonstrated that a real story, told through the strong vehicle of video, could lift a brand from lack of clarity to unmistakable quality.

# Overview of Video Marketing

Video showcasing is a dynamic and strong system that uses the notoriety and viability of recordings to advance items, administrations, or brands. In the present computerized age, where capacities to focus are contracting and visual quality writing is everything, video showcasing has arisen as a vital device for organizations to interface with their main interest group. This outline dives into the vital parts of video showcasing, investigating its advantages, types, best practices, and the developing scene.

**Advantages of Video Showcasing:**
**Commitment and Consideration:**
Video content dazzles crowds more successfully than text or pictures. The mix of visuals, sound, and narrating makes it simpler for watchers to draw in with and hold data.
**Increased Revenue:**

Concentrates reliably show that adding a video to a presentation page can fundamentally help change rates. Whether it's an item show or a convincing brand story, recordings have the ability to change over watchers into clients.

**Website design enhancement Lift:**
Web search tools love video content. Videos on websites have a greater chance of appearing higher in search results. This can work on a brand's perceivability and draw in natural rush hour gridlock.

**Reach on Social Media:**
Online entertainment stages focus on video content, making it bound to show up in clients' feeds. This assists in expanding reach and commitment on stages with loving Facebook, Instagram, and Twitter.

**Versatility:**
Video marketing is adaptable and can take many forms, including testimonials, live streams, explainer videos, product demonstrations, and more. This flexibility permits organizations to fit their video content to various phases of the client venture.

**Kinds of Video Showcasing:**
**Video Tutorials:**
The purpose of these brief videos is to provide an engaging and straightforward explanation of a product, service, or idea. They are perfect for acquainting new contributions with the crowd.

**Item Exhibits:**
Showing an item in real life assists expected clients with grasping its highlights and advantages. This kind of video can improve the general shopping experience.

**Tributes and Contextual analyses:**
Testimonials and success stories from actual people increase credibility and trust. Hearing fulfilled clients share their encounters can impact others to make a buy.

**Live Recordings:**
Live gushing on stages like Facebook Live or Instagram Live gives a chance to continuous collaboration with the crowd. It tends to be utilized for item dispatches, interactive discussions, or in the background looks.

**Vivified Recordings:**
Vivified recordings are outwardly engaging and can work on complex thoughts. They are especially helpful for organizations managing dynamic or theoretical items.

**Best Practices in Video Advertising:**

**Grasp Your Crowd:**
Tailor your recordings to your interest group's inclinations and interests. Understanding your crowd's socioeconomics and ways of behaving can direct the substance creation process.

**Advance for Portable:**
Video optimization for mobile viewing is essential given the rising popularity of smartphones. Guarantee that your recordings are effectively open and give a consistent encounter on different gadgets.

**Recount a Convincing Story:**
Narrating adds a close to home layer to your recordings, making them more important. Create a story that resounds with your crowd and imparts your image's qualities.

**Keep it Succinct:**

Abilities to focus are short, so plan to effectively convey your message. Go for the gold keeping up with clearness and effect.

## Quality Matters:

Put money into high-quality video production. Clear visuals and top notch sound add to an expert and reliable picture.

## Advancing Scene of Video Promoting:

## Intuitive Recordings:

The eventual fate of video advertising incorporates intuitive components like interactive areas of interest, tests, and overviews inside recordings. As a result, viewers become active participants rather than passive observers.

## Computer-generated reality (VR) and expanded reality (AR):

AR and VR innovations are progressively
incorporated into video promoting, offering vivid and intelligent encounters. This pattern is probably going to develop as these advances become more open.

## Short-Structure Recordings:

Stages like TikTok and Instagram Reels have promoted short-structure recordings. To meet the needs of users with limited time, brands are responding to this trend by producing content that is condensed and compelling.

## Personalization:

High level information examination empowers customized video content in light of client inclinations and conduct. Fitting recordings to individual watchers can fundamentally improve commitment and change rates.

All in all, video promoting keeps on being a dynamic and fundamental part of a far reaching computerized showcasing technique. Its capacity to spellbind crowds, help commitment, and drive transformations makes it a useful asset for organizations across enterprises. By keeping up to date with advancing patterns and consolidating best practices, organizations can tackle the maximum capacity of video promoting to associate with their crowd in significant ways.

# Importance of Video Content for Brand Awareness

In today's digital landscape, video content plays a crucial role in shaping and increasing brand awareness. As buyers progressively go to online stages for data and amusement, the significance of utilizing video couldn't possibly be more significant. From online entertainment to sites, video content has turned into a flexible and drawing in device for brands to interface with their crowd. The following are a few key viewpoints featuring the meaning of video content for brand mindfulness:

**1. Visual Effect and Narrating:**
Video content gives a dynamic and outwardly convincing method for recounting a brand's story. Through a mix of visuals, sound, and story, brands

can make a significant and sincerely full insight for their crowd. This narrating approach assists with refining the brand, making it engaging and laying out a more profound association with watchers.

## 2. Expanded Commitment:

Recordings catch consideration more successfully than text or static pictures. The human mind processes visual data quicker, and recordings can pass on a message in a limited capacity to focus. Subsequently, customers are bound to draw in with video content, prompting expanded mindfulness and a higher probability of sharing the substance inside their organizations.

## 3. Virtual Entertainment Strength:

Online entertainment stages have developed into content utilization centers, and recordings become the overwhelming focus. Platforms like Facebook, Instagram, and TikTok make it easy for users to engage with video content by providing features like autoplay and video previews. Brands that decisively influence video on these stages can take advantage of immense client bases and upgrade their perceivability.

## 4. Site design improvement (Search engine optimization):

Web crawlers favor video content, and sites highlighting recordings frequently rank higher in list items. Remembering recordings for a site upgrades its Website design enhancement, driving more natural traffic. This, in turn, makes the brand more visible and makes it easier for potential customers to find out about it.

## 5. Instructive Substance and Authority Building:

Video content permits brands to share instructive and useful material. Whether through instructional exercises, item exhibitions, or master interviews, brands can situate themselves as industry specialists. This forms entrust with the crowd as well as lays out the brand as a go-to hotspot for important data, building up brand mindfulness.

## 6. Consistency across devices:

When building a brand, consistency is essential. Brands can maintain a consistent message across platforms with video content. A well-thought-out video strategy keeps the brand's identity consistent across all platforms, including YouTube, Instagram, and the company's website, making it easier for audiences of all kinds to recognize it.

## 7. Shareability and Virality:

Video content has a higher probability of turning into a web sensation contrasted with different sorts of content. Drawing in and shareable recordings can rapidly contact a huge crowd as watchers share happiness with their organizations. This natural sharing widens brand mindfulness as well as acquaints the brand with new crowds.

## 8. Portable Availability:

With the predominance of cell phones, buyers are consuming substances in a hurry. Video content is profoundly available on cell phones, permitting brands to contact crowds any place they are. The comfort of versatile survey upgrades the possibilities of clients drawing in with the substance and recollecting the brand.

## 9. Adapting to Change:

Video content adjusts well to the latest things and organizations. To stay relevant and attract a wider audience, brands can make use of popular video challenges, formats, or trends. Being versatile and lining up with contemporary video patterns guarantees that the brand stays noticeable and reverberates with the advancing inclinations of customers.

**10. Measurements and Investigation:**
*(css Duplicate code)*

*Video stages give powerful examination instruments, permitting brands to gauge the viability of their substance. Measurements, for example, sees, watch time, and commitment rates offer important bits of knowledge into crowd conduct. Brands can utilize this information to refine their video methodology, guaranteeing that future substance is custom fitted to reverberate with their ideal interest group.*

All in all, the significance of video content for brand mindfulness couldn't possibly be more significant in the computerized age. From cultivating commitment to building authority and utilizing the fame of virtual entertainment, video content has turned into a foundation of fruitful brand correspondence. By embracing the force of visual narrating, brands can make an enduring effect on their crowd, set their character, and remain at the forefront of purchaser mindfulness.

# Chapter 1 Understanding Your Audience

Understanding your crowd is fundamental in the domain of video showcasing, as it establishes the groundwork for making content that resounds and connects really. An effective video showcasing system depends on a profound perception of who your crowd is, what they are worth, and how they consume content.

Socioeconomics, first and foremost, assume a vital part in crowd understanding. Your video content can be tailored to the preferences of your target audience by analyzing factors like age, gender, location, and occupation. For example, a video focusing on youngsters could consolidate energetic visuals, stylish music, and interesting subjects, while content for experts might embrace a more cleaned and useful tone.

Besides, psychographics dive into the mental parts of your crowd. Grasping their inclinations, side interests, and way of life decisions empowers you to make recordings that hit home on an individual level. For example, assuming that your crowd is naturally cognizant, consolidating eco-accommodating practices in your recordings can improve their allure. By lining up with your crowd's qualities, you lay out a more profound association that rises above a simple conditional relationship.

Besides, understanding the way of behaving and the inclinations of your crowd is fundamental. Breaking down information on how they consume content, like favored stages, gadget use, and review designs, permits you to streamline your video advertising technique. For example, in the event that your crowd is overwhelmingly dynamic via online entertainment, creating more limited, shareable recordings might be more powerful. Alternatively, assuming that they like top to bottom data, longer-structure recordings on stages like YouTube may be more reasonable.

Past socioeconomics and psychographics, making purchaser personas can give an extensive comprehension of your crowd. You can tailor your content to meet the needs, challenges, and preferences of each segment of your audience by creating fictional characters who represent them. This customized approach upgrades the pertinence of your recordings, making them more convincing to your interest group.

Presently, we should dive into the universe of video promotion. Video has turned into a predominant power in computerized advertising because of its capacity to pass on data in an outwardly convincing and connecting way. From limited time content to instructive instructional exercises, the adaptability of video permits brands to interface with their crowd on different levels.

One of the critical benefits of video promoting is its ability to inspire feelings. Whether it's through narrating, music, or visuals, recordings can get close to home reactions that reverberate with watchers. Brand loyalty and audience retention are both enhanced by this emotional connection. By understanding the close to home triggers of your crowd, you can make recordings that leave an enduring effect.

Furthermore, video content has a higher degree of consistency contrasted with different types of media. The mix of sound and visual components makes it more straightforward for watchers to assimilate and recall data. This maintenance power is important in passing on complex messages, exhibiting item includes, or conveying noteworthy brand messages. Utilizing the visual and hear-able faculties guarantees that your substance stays in the personalities of your crowd for a more expanded period.

Additionally, video marketing expands its reach and accessibility. With the expansion of cell phones and high velocity web, recordings can be effortlessly gotten to by a worldwide crowd. Stages like YouTube, Instagram, and TikTok give a tremendous stage to brands to feature their substance. The capacity to contact a different and far reaching crowd is a strong part of video promoting, permitting brands to rise above geological limits and social contrasts.

The intelligent idea of video content additionally adds to its adequacy.

Highlights like remarks, likes, and offers work with commitment, transforming uninvolved watchers into dynamic members. This collaboration fabricates a local area around your image as well as gives important experiences into crowd inclinations and opinions. Checking these associations empowers you to adjust and refine your video promoting system in view of ongoing criticism.

Ultimately, the ascent of video website streamlining (VSEO) underlines the significance of recordings in web search tool rankings. Video content is favored by search engines, and videos that are optimized well can significantly increase your website's visibility. Creating convincing video titles, depictions, and labels with applicable catchphrases guarantees that your substance is discoverable by your ideal interest group.

All in all, understanding your crowd is the foundation of a fruitful video showcasing methodology. You can personalize your videos to resonate with your target audience by delving into demographics, psychographics, behavior, and preferences. Video promoting, with its personal effect, high consistency standard, openness, intelligence, and Web optimization benefits, gives a dynamic and successful method for drawing in and extending your crowd in the computerized scene.

# Target Audience Analysis

Understanding your interest group is vital for effective showcasing systems, and in the domain of computerized promoting, video content has arisen as an integral asset to draw in and interface with crowds. We should dive into the meaning of main interest group investigation and its crossing point with video promotion.

**Interest group Examination:**

Main interest group examination includes contemplating and grasping the socioeconomics, interests, ways of behaving, and needs of the gathering you need to reach. This cycle is fundamental since it helps tailor showcasing endeavors to reverberate with the particular inclinations of the crowd, expanding the possibilities of transformation.

**Demographics:**

Knowing the age, orientation, area, pay level, and instruction of your crowd gives a fundamental comprehension. For example, an item focusing on teens will require an alternate showcasing approach than one taking care of moderately aged experts.

**Psychographics:**

Digging into the mental parts of your crowd, like qualities, interests, leisure activities, and way of life, makes content that lines up with their convictions and inclinations. This more profound comprehension empowers the improvement of more customized and appealing promoting efforts.

**Social Bits of knowledge:**

Dissecting buyer conduct, including buying designs, online propensities, and reaction to advertising improvements, expects their necessities and inclinations. This information is instrumental in making focused and powerful messages.

**Needs and Problem areas:**

Distinguishing the necessities and trouble spots of your crowd permits you to situate your item or administration as an answer. Tending to these worries straightforwardly in your promoting content cultivates a feeling of understanding and association.

**Video Advertising:**

Video promoting has turned into a prevailing power in the computerized scene, with stages like YouTube, TikTok, and Instagram utilizing the force of visual substance to draw in crowds. Video marketing's effectiveness and compatibility with target audience analysis are as follows:

**Visual Allure:**

People are normally attracted to visual boosts. Recordings catch consideration more really than text or static pictures. Drawing in visuals can pass on data in a really convincing and paramount manner, making your message stay with the crowd.

**Narrating Valuable open doors:**

Recordings give a unique stage to narrating. By winding around stories that resound with your crowd's encounters and feelings, you can make a more profound association and have an enduring effect. The psychographic aspect of target audience analysis is in line with this.

**Versatility:**

Video content comes in different structures - from short clasps to longer stories, live streams to movements. This flexibility permits advertisers to pick the arrangement that best suits their main interest group and showcasing objectives. For example, more youthful crowds could answer well to short, smart recordings on stages like TikTok.

**Virtual Entertainment Mix:**

Online entertainment stages intensely focus on video content, with calculations frequently inclining toward recordings over different sorts of posts. Meeting your audience where they spend their online time is in line with the behavioral insights gleaned from target audience analysis.

**Website optimization Advantages:**

Video content upgrades your site's website improvement (Web optimization). Web search tools progressively focus on video results, and by making applicable, top notch recordings, you can work on your site's perceivability and draw in natural rush hour gridlock.

**The Advantageous interaction of Interest group Investigation and Video Advertising:**

**Custom fitted Substance:**

By understanding your main interest group's inclinations, you can make recordings that talk straightforwardly to their inclinations and resonate with their qualities. This custom fitted methodology improves the probability of commitment and transformation.

**Personalization:**

Video advertising considers customized content encounters. You can create videos with personalized messaging that address specific needs and concerns of various segments of your audience by utilizing data from a target audience analysis.

**Proper communication:**

You can communicate more effectively when you know who your target audience is. Whether it's utilizing humor, close to home requests, or instructive substance, adjusting your video informing with the inclinations of your crowd guarantees that your message resounds.

**Input Circles:**

Video investigation gives important experiences into crowd conduct. By investigating measurements like watch time, navigate rates, and watcher socioeconomics, you can refine how you might interpret your crowd over the long run, persistently further developing your video showcasing methodology.

All in all, main interest group examination and video showcasing are indivisible parts of a fruitful computerized promoting system. Understanding your crowd advises the creation regarding convincing and pertinent video content, while video showcasing, thusly, takes into account dynamic and drawing in correspondence with that crowd. This harmonious relationship upgrades brand perceivability as well as cultivates enduring associations among organizations and their objective shoppers.

# Tailoring Video Content to Audience Preferences

A strategic strategy that can significantly affect the success of any video-based platform or marketing campaign is to tailor video content to audience preferences. In the present advanced age, where abilities to focus are passing and contest for watcher commitment is serious, understanding and taking special care of the inclinations of your interest group is significant.

Above all else, distinguishing the socioeconomics of your crowd is central. Age, orientation, area, and interests assume a crucial part in forming content inclinations. For example, a more youthful crowd might incline towards short, outwardly captivating recordings with an energetic feel, while a more established segment could favor more top to bottom, enlightening substance. By examining these variables, content makers can create recordings that resonate with their particular crowd, improving the probability of catching and holding their consideration.

Outside socioeconomics, the ability to comprehend the psychographics of the crowd is similarly fundamental. Psychographics envelop the mental parts of people, like qualities, perspectives, interests, and ways of life. Content that more closely reflects the preferences of the audience can be produced with this deeper comprehension. For instance, an educated crowd might see the value in satisfaction that investigates state of the art developments, while an ecologically cognizant crowd might lean toward recordings underlining supportable practices.

In addition, platforms are essential for customizing video content. The behaviors and expectations of each audience are different on different platforms. For example, TikTok flourishes with short, smart recordings customized for fast utilization, while YouTube considers longer-structure content taking special care of watchers looking for more top to bottom data. Adjusting content to fit the remarkable highlights and necessities of every stage guarantees greatest reach and commitment.

Personalization is one more key part of fitting video content. Content creators can provide personalized recommendations by analyzing viewer preferences and behavior with the help of data analytics and AI algorithms. This improves the watcher's insight as well as improves the probability of them drawing in with comparable substance later on. Personalization makes a feeling of association, causing the crowd to feel comprehended and esteemed.

Besides, remaining receptive to the latest things is crucial in fitting video content successfully. Patterns are always advancing, and adjusting content to what's presently well known can draw in additional perspectives and offers. This doesn't mean indiscriminately pursuing directions yet rather understanding them and incorporating components that resound with the main interest group. This flexibility guarantees that the substance stays applicable and engaging after some time.

Commitment is a two-way road, and integrating intelligent components into video content can upgrade the watcher experience. Highlights like surveys, tests, and source of inspiration prompts support crowd investment, transforming aloof watchers into dynamic benefactors. This not just fortifies the association between the substance maker and the crowd yet in addition gives important bits of knowledge into crowd inclinations.

Openness is a basic thought in fitting video content. It is essential to ensure that the content is accessible to a diverse audience and easy to comprehend. Using clear language, providing subtitles for those who are hard of hearing, and creating content that crosses cultural and linguistic boundaries are all part of this. A generally open video takes care of a more extensive crowd, expanding its effect.

Consistency in informing and marking adds to building major areas of strength for a with the crowd. A sense of familiarity and trust are cultivated when viewers notice a consistent style, tone, or theme across videos. This doesn't mean each video ought to be indistinguishable, yet keeping a durable brand personality guarantees that the crowd knows what's in store and can undoubtedly associate with the substance.

Understanding demographics, psychographics, platform dynamics, and current trends is essential when tailoring video content to audience preferences. By customizing content, remaining intelligent, and guaranteeing openness and consistency, content makers could not just catch the consideration of their interest group at any point yet in addition cultivate an enduring association. In the unique scene of computerized content, adjusting and developing with crowd inclinations is the way to support achievement.

# Chapter 2 Creating Compelling Video Content

Making convincing video content is fundamental in the present advanced scene, where capacities to focus are short, and rivalry for watchers is savage. Understanding the essential components of creating engaging videos can make a significant difference in capturing and keeping your audience's attention, regardless of whether you are a content creator, marketer, or business owner.

**Grasping Your Crowd**

Prior to jumping into the innovative approach, knowing your interest group is pivotal.What are their tendencies,

tendencies, and pain points? Fitting your substance to resound with your crowd improves the probability of them drawing in with your recordings. Directing reviews, investigating virtual entertainment socioeconomics, and contemplating examination can give important bits of knowledge into your crowd's inclinations.

## Characterizing Your Message

Each convincing video starts with a reasonable and succinct message. Whether you're delivering information, telling a story, or promoting a product, it's important to clearly communicate your message from the beginning. Keep away from vagueness and guarantee that your crowd grasps the reason for your video inside the initial couple of moments. This lucidity establishes the vibe for the whole survey insight.

## Captivating Thumbnails and Titles

In the world of video content, thumbnails and titles are your front door. First impressions matter. Make a thumbnail that sticks out and precisely addresses the substance. It should be interesting, relevant, and visually appealing. Similarly, your title ought to be compact, convincing, and incorporate important catchphrases for inquiry streamlining.

## Connecting with Narrating

Successful narrating is the foundation of convincing video content. Make a story that reverberates with your crowd inwardly. Whether it's through humor, show, or motivation, a very much recounted story spellbinds watchers and keeps them put resources into the video. Utilize an organized methodology with an unmistakable start, center, and end to keep a smooth stream.

## Visual Allure and Creation Quality

Quality matters, and this is particularly valid for video content. To improve the overall quality of the production, spend money on high-quality camera gear, lighting, and sound. Spotless, sufficiently bright shots with clear sound add to an expert and charming survey insight. Post-production attention to detail, including graphics and editing, improves the visual appeal of your videos.

## Compact and Centered Content

In the period of limited ability to focus, keeping your substance brief and centered is significant. Keep away from superfluous cushions and quit wasting time. In the event that your video requires a more extended term, think about breaking it into edible sections or parts. Keep a harmony between giving important data and keeping the crowd connected all through the video.

## Integrating Visual Assortment

To forestall watcher exhaustion, integrate visual assortment into your recordings. This incorporates a blend of shots, changes, and illustrations to keep the substance outwardly invigorating. Try different things with various camera points, use liveliness or illustrations to underline central issues, and influence B-roll film to supplement your account. A dynamic and engaging viewing experience is the objective.

## Using Music and Audio cues

Music effectively affects the close to home tone of your video. Pick ambient sound that supplements the mind-set and message you need to pass on. Also, essential utilization of audio effects can improve explicit minutes, adding profundity and inundation to the watcher's insight. Guarantee that sound levels are adjusted to try not to overpower or diverting the crowd.

## Intuitiveness and Source of inspiration

Support watcher commitment by integrating intelligent components into your recordings. Suggest conversation starters, gather information, or incorporate interactive components that lead to extra happy or significant sites. Furthermore, obviously convey a source of inspiration (CTA) to direct watchers on the subsequent stages, whether it's buying into your channel, visiting your site, or making a buy.

## Optimizing for Search and Accessibility

Make your video content as search engine friendly as possible. Utilize applicable catchphrases in your video title, portrayal, and labels. Make a drawing in video depiction that gives extra setting and incorporates significant connections. Add closed captions or subtitles to your videos to make them accessible to a wider audience and enhance the overall user experience.

## Consistency and Marking

Building a devoted crowd requires consistency in both substance and marking. Lay out a conspicuous style for your recordings, including predictable variety plans, textual styles, and illustrations. This durable visual personality assists watchers with distinguishing your substance rapidly and cultivates a feeling of commonality. Furthermore, keep a normal presenting plan on keep your crowd connected with and expecting new happy.

All in all, making convincing video content requires a smart mix of imagination, specialized mastery, and grasping your crowd. By zeroing in on clear informing, connecting with narrating, visual allure, and intuitiveness, you can deliver recordings that catch and hold the consideration of your main interest group. In the ever-changing digital landscape, your video content must remain compelling and relevant by remaining consistent, adapting to trends, and continually refining your strategy in response to feedback from your audience.

# Storytelling Techniques

Narrating is a workmanship that has enamored mankind for quite a long time, rising above social limits and developing with the progression of time. The methods of telling a story have changed and grown over time, from ancient oral traditions to modern multimedia platforms, resulting in a diverse collection of narrative styles. Whether it's writing, film, or even a straightforward discussion, compelling narrating methods are fundamental for drawing in crowds and passing on messages with influence.

One major narrating strategy is the foundation of a convincing story structure. A very much created story regularly follows a three-act structure, consisting of composition, rising activity, peak, falling activity, and goal. The storyteller can use this framework as a road map to ensure a logical progression that keeps the audience invested. In any case, inside this design lies adequate space for imagination; nonlinear accounts, flashbacks, or resemble storylines can add intricacy and interest.

Another crucial aspect of storytelling is character growth. Vital characters are the core of any account, and their development or change all through the story resounds with crowds. Methods, for example, "show, don't tell" empower the crowd to interface with characters on a more profound level by noticing their activities, contemplations, and feelings. Also, presenting defects, struggles under the surface, and individual stakes can make characters more interesting and three-layered.

The specialty of pacing is a sensitive yet imperative narrating strategy. Controlling the beat of a story guarantees that strain, fervor, and profound effect are conveyed at vital places. A dynamic narrative is made possible by well-timed revelations, plot twists, and moments of reflection. A skilled storyteller uses time manipulation to keep the audience engaged, whether they speed up action sequences or slow down character development.

Symbolism and tactile subtleties assume an essential part in shipping crowds to the story's reality. Distinctive portrayals that enticement for the faculties make a more vivid encounter. By portraying the setting, characters, and occasions, narrators manufacture an association between the story and the crowd's creative mind. Analogies, comparisons, and imagery can additionally improve the profundity and wealth of the narrating woven artwork.

Successful discourse is a useful asset for passing on data, uncovering character qualities, and propelling the plot. Normal sounding discourse reflects genuine discussions and cultivates a feeling of realness. Subtext, the implicit subtleties underneath the outer layer of words, adds intricacy to character associations. Additionally, sensible utilization of exchange labels, stops, and varieties in tone adds to the general mood and stream of the story.

Vital utilization of contention is basic to keeping up with crowd interest. Whether it's conflicts under the surface inside a person or outside challenges presented by the plot, struggle is the motor that drives the story forward. Strain and anticipation are uplifted when hindrances and obstructions ceaselessly defeat the hero's objectives. Settling clashes sufficiently gives a feeling of conclusion while leaving space for expected spin-offs or future turns of events.

Joseph Campbell popularized the hero's journey concept, which outlines a common narrative structure that transcends cultures and time periods. This monomyth structure includes a legend wandering into the obscure, confronting difficulties, going through change, and getting back different. Narrators frequently consolidate varieties of this prototype excursion to make a story that takes advantage of major human encounters and desires.

Powerful narrating likewise includes grasping the ideal interest group and fitting the account appropriately. Social references, language decisions, and topical components ought to line up with the expected segment. Whether making a kids' story or an experienced show, the narrating methods utilized ought to take care of the sensibilities and assumptions for the crowd, encouraging a more grounded association.

The component of shock, accomplished through unexpected developments and startling turns of events, adds an additional layer of energy to narrating. While hinting can quietly set up the crowd for impending disclosures, a top notch wind can undermine assumptions, leaving an enduring effect. The delicate art of balancing predictability and unpredictability is what keeps the audience interested and guessing.

In the computerized age, media narrating has acquainted new aspects with the art. Visual narration in film and TV, intelligent narrating in computer games, and vivid narrating in augmented experience push the limits of conventional account structures. Utilizing these mediums requires a comprehension of their remarkable abilities and imperatives, empowering narrators to make convincing encounters across different stages.

All in all, narrating methods are the strings that mesh stories into embroideries of feeling, creative mind, and importance. From the construction and pacing to character improvement and struggle, each component adds to the general effect of a story. Whether told around a pit fire, written in a book, or portrayed on a screen, stories have the ability to engage, teach, and motivate, making narrating a persevering and fundamental part of the human experience.

# Visual and Audio Elements

Visual and sound components assume a pivotal part in molding our encounters, whether in the domain of diversion, correspondence, or craftsmanship. These aspects have the ability to captivate, elicit feelings, and communicate intricate ideas. For creating content that is both immersive and impactful, it is essential to comprehend how the visual and audio components interact with one another.

In the domain of film, the marriage of visual and sound components is obvious in each edge. The visual foundation of a movie is laid by cinematography, which includes things like framing, composition, and lighting. These components work coupled with the heart-able parts, like audio effects, music, and exchange, to make a tangible orchestra that directs the watcher through a story venture. A very much created scene use the synchronicity of visuals and sound to escalate feelings and support narrating.

Consider the exemplary shower scene from Alfred Hitchcock's "Psycho." The obvious, high-contrast high contrast visuals, joined with Bernard Herrmann's famous shrieking violin score, make a climate of strain and dread. The shower scene is a demonstration of the cooperative effect of visual and sound components, showing the way that the marriage of chilling symbolism and tormenting music can scratch a permanent blemish on the watcher's mind.

In the domain of promoting, visual and sound components are decisively utilized to have an enduring effect. To increase brand recall, advertisements, for instance, make use of catchy jingles and visually engaging images. The cooperative energy between what is seen and what is heard in these commercials means to make a comprehensive tangible encounter, supporting the item or message in the watcher's memory. Consider promoting jingles like McDonald's "I'm Lovin' It" or Intel's five-note jingle — these sound components become indivisible from the visual marking, laying out a firm character for the brand.

Moving past the screen, the meaning of visual and sound components stretches out to the domain of computer generated reality (VR). In VR encounters, the combination of reasonable visuals and spatial sound is crucial for making a feeling of presence. A virtual climate turns out to be more vivid when the visuals adjust consistently with the directional prompts given by sound. For example, in a VR recreation of a woodland, the stirring leaves ought to spatially relate with the visual portrayal, upgrading the client's view of being encircled ordinarily.

In the realm of gaming, visual and sound components are vital to interactivity and account drenching. Excellent illustrations, complicated movements, and nitty gritty surfaces add to the visual allure of a game, while dynamic audio effects and a convincing melodic score improve the general gaming experience. Effective games wonderfully interweave these components to make a firm and drawing world for players to investigate.

Think about the ghastliness kind in gaming, where the mix of ghostly visuals and tormenting sound plan is utilized to prompt apprehension and tension. A well-timed creaking door or distant footsteps can increase tension and add excitement to the gaming experience. On the other hand, in experience games, elevating visuals matched with a motivating melodic score can summon a feeling of stunningness and wonder, improving the player's association with the virtual world.

With regards to live exhibitions, visual and sound components add to the general effect of shows, theater creations, and different occasions. To enhance the auditory experience, the lighting design, stage setup, and visual effects are carefully orchestrated. For instance, not only does a live musical performance benefit from the talent of the musicians, but stage lighting and projections also add to the spectacle.

In addition, visual and sound components are significant in instructive settings. Instructive recordings, introductions, and e-learning modules influence visuals to pass on data actually, while sound components, for example, portrayal or ambient sound can improve commitment and maintenance. The mix of convincing visuals and clear sound works with a more vivid and compelling opportunity for growth.

Taking everything into account, the multifaceted dance among visual and sound components shapes our experiences with different types of media and diversion. Whether in film, promoting, computer generated reality, gaming, live exhibitions, or schooling, the joint effort of visuals and sound makes a multi-tangible encounter that resounds with crowds. For creators who want to produce content that not only piques the audience's interest but also leaves a lasting impression on the senses, it is essential to comprehend the symbiotic relationship that exists between these components.

# Length and Format Considerations

Length and organization contemplations assume an urgent part in different parts of correspondence, going from scholarly papers to business reports and exploratory writing. Finding some kind of harmony between these components is fundamental for passing on data successfully and connecting with the crowd. Whether it's a brief article or a broad exploration paper, understanding the subtleties of length and configuration is fundamental for fruitful correspondence.

In scholastic composition, sticking to explicit length prerequisites is many times a central perspective. Teachers and diaries might give rules that direct the OK scope of words or pages for a given task. Meeting these rules isn't just a question of consistency yet additionally mirrors the capacity to introduce data briefly and rationally. Excessive verbosity or a lack of depth can detract from the overall quality of the work if the length is skewed too far from the required minimum.

Nonetheless, the significance of length goes past simple word count. It reaches out to the design of the substance, including the presentation, body, and end. A powerful presentation ought to be compact, catching the pursuer's consideration and giving a reasonable outline of the subject. The body ought to dig into the central matters, keeping a consistent stream and keeping away from pointless redundancy. A brief end ought to sum up key discoveries and have an enduring effect. Finding some kind of harmony among profundity and quickness in each segment adds to a very much organized and drawing in piece.

In the domain of business correspondence, the length and organization of reports, recommendations, and introductions are basic for passing data on to partners. Business environments frequently feature time constraints, making it essential to present information in a clear and concise manner. Reports that are too extended might be ignored or skimmed, prompting a deficiency of key subtleties. Conversely, communications that are overly succinct may not provide the necessary depth for comprehensive comprehension.

The organization of business archives is similarly huge. Using headings, list items, and visual components can upgrade clarity and work with data recovery. An efficient organization guarantees that the crowd can rapidly get a handle on the central matters and explore through the substance effectively. The use of visuals like charts and graphs in presentations can help reinforce key points and complement the spoken word. Finding some kind of harmony among text and visuals is pivotal for keeping up with crowd commitment.

Experimental writing, while frequently bearing the cost of additional adaptability as far as length and arrangement, actually requires conscious thought. Brief tales request succinctness and accuracy, expecting creators to convey a convincing story inside a restricted word count. Books, then again, consider a greater investigation of characters, subjects, and plotlines. For readers to remain engaged, chapters must be balanced in length and the structure must remain consistent.

Design contemplations in exploratory writing stretch out to style, tone, and pacing. The reader's experience can be influenced by the font, spacing, and alignment that are chosen. Consistency in designing adds to a cleaned and proficient appearance, whether in a composition or a distributed book. Understanding the shows of the picked classification is additionally essential; for instance, a screenplay follows an unexpected configuration in comparison to a book.

In computerized correspondence, for example, blog entries or online entertainment content, capacities to focus are in many cases more limited, requesting a succinct and drawing in approach. Breaking up the text and making it easier to read are subheadings, bullet points, and multimedia elements. The utilization of hyperlinks can guide users to extra data, keeping up with curtness while giving chances to additional investigation.

All in all, length and arrangement contemplations are essential to successful correspondence across different spaces. Whether in scholar, business, or imaginative settings, understanding the crowd and object is critical to finding some kind of harmony. Complying with rules while keeping an unmistakable and drawing in structure guarantees that the planned message is passed on with influence. Whether you're writing a creative essay, a business report, or a research paper, the secret to good communication is knowing how to navigate the complicated relationship between length and format.

# Chapter 3
# Platforms and Distribution Strategies

Businesses in a variety of sectors rely heavily on distribution strategies and platforms to succeed. In the contemporary computerized scene, the expression "stage" has developed past its customary importance, enveloping an expansive range of online spaces where organizations associate with their crowd. The choice of a company's platform and distribution strategy can have a significant impact on its reach, revenue, and overall success, regardless of whether the platform is an e-commerce platform, a social media network, or a streaming service.

Businesses looking to enter the vast online market now require ecommerce platforms. Organizations like Amazon, Shopify, and eBay give a virtual commercial center where merchants can feature and offer their items to a worldwide crowd. The nature of the products, target audience, and desired level of customization are all important considerations when selecting an e-commerce platform. For example, a little high quality specialties business could flourish with a stage like Etsy, known for its emphasis on interesting, distinctive items, while a tech contraption retailer might incline toward a stage with a more extensive client base like Amazon.

Online entertainment stages have additionally arisen as useful assets for organizations to interface with their crowd. Stages like Facebook, Instagram, Twitter, and LinkedIn offer interesting open doors for organizations to draw in with their clients, assemble brand mindfulness, and even drive deals. The decision of virtual entertainment stages relies upon the objective segment and the sort of satisfaction the business needs to share. Instagram may be successful for businesses focused on visuals, whereas

LinkedIn may be preferred by B2B businesses for professional networking.

In the domain of content creation and utilization, streaming stages have reformed the manner in which we access music, films, and Network programs. Administrations like Spotify, Netflix, and Disney+ have upset customary circulation models, permitting clients to appreciate content on-request. The progress of a streaming stage frequently depends on its substance library, client experience, and valuing technique. Platforms are heavily investing in exclusive shows and movies to attract and retain subscribers, making original content production a key differentiator.

In addition, the expansion of the app ecosystem has opened up new avenues for businesses to directly interact with customers via smartphones and tablets. Application circulation stages like the Apple Application Store and Google Play Store act as doors for engineers to disseminate their versatile applications to a worldwide crowd. An app's success often depends on its functionality, user interface, and marketing strategies that work. Successive updates and responsiveness to client criticism are essential for keeping a positive client experience.

It becomes increasingly important for businesses to develop an efficient distribution strategy as they navigate the numerous platforms. Due to the fact that it enables businesses to reach a larger audience, the omnichannel strategy, which involves utilizing multiple platforms simultaneously, has gained popularity. Notwithstanding, this approach requires cautious coordination to guarantee a predictable brand picture and consistent client experience across various stages.

The direct-to-buyer (DTC) model has additionally acquired ubiquity, empowering organizations to sell their items or administrations straightforwardly to clients without go-betweens. The customer experience, data, and pricing are all under greater control with this strategy. DTC marks frequently influence internet business stages, virtual entertainment, and their sites to lay out an immediate association with buyers.

Moreover, organizations and joint efforts among organizations and stages can be an essential dispersion strategy. Companies can benefit from the platform's marketing reach and leverage existing user bases by joining established platforms. For instance, a style brand teaming up with a well known web-based commercial center can acquire openness to a more extensive crowd and possibly drive deals through the laid out stage's client trust.

Be that as it may, the powerful idea of the computerized scene additionally presents difficulties for organizations. Mechanical headways, changing customer ways of behaving, and developing stage arrangements require flexibility. For long-term success, it's important to keep up with industry trends and evaluate platforms' performance on a regular basis.

Taking everything into account, stages and circulation systems are vital parts of present day business tasks. The choice of platforms has a significant impact on a company's success and reach, whether through e-commerce, social media, streaming services, or mobile apps. Creating a compelling appropriation procedure includes figuring out the ideal interest group, utilizing numerous channels, and adjusting to the developing computerized scene.

Organizations that explore this territory decisively are better situated to flourish in an undeniably interconnected and serious worldwide market.

# Choosing the Right Platforms

Picking the right stages is a pivotal choice for people and organizations the same in the present computerized age. With an ever growing cluster of online stages accessible, going from web-based entertainment to internet business, pursuing informed decisions can fundamentally affect one's prosperity. The determination interaction includes thinking about different variables, including the ideal interest group, objectives, and the idea of the substance or items being advertised.

To begin, recognizing the ideal interest group is vital. Various stages draw in unmistakable socioeconomics and client ways of behaving. For example, in the event that the point is to interface with a more youthful crowd, stages like Instagram and TikTok may be more compelling. Then again, in the event that the objective is to arrive at experts or take part in B2B exercises, LinkedIn could be the favored decision. Understanding the socioeconomics and inclinations of the target group is fundamental for fitting substance and correspondence techniques successfully.

Then, characterizing explicit objectives is fundamental in directing stage determination. Do you want to foster community engagement, increase sales, or raise brand awareness? Every stage has its assets, and adjusting your objectives to these qualities is critical. For brand mindfulness, outwardly determined stages like Instagram or Pinterest may be reasonable, while web based business objectives might be ideally serviced by stages with coordinated shopping highlights, like Facebook or Shopify.

Thought ought to likewise be given to the idea of the substance or items being advertised. For example, assuming your business depends intensely on visual allure, stages like YouTube or Instagram, which focus on visual substance, could be profitable. On the other hand, platforms like Twitter or LinkedIn might be better suited to your content if it is more informational or text-based.

Additionally, it is essential to evaluate the competition and industry standards across a variety of platforms. Understanding where contenders are dynamic and where your ideal interest group is most drawn in can give important experiences. Not all platforms require one to be present; all things being equal, zeroing in on the ones where your rivals are fruitful and your crowd is dynamic can yield improved results.

Moreover, the degree of commitment and association wanted ought to impact stage decisions. Facebook Groups and Reddit, for example, provide more opportunities for direct interaction and community building than others. Others might be more qualified for broadcasting updates or sharing substance, similar to Twitter. Evaluating the ideal degree of commitment can assist in deciding the stages that line up with your correspondence methodology.

Budgetary considerations are another important factor. While numerous stages offer free access, a few highlights or promoting choices might require extra speculation. Organizations ought to gauge the expected profit from venture against the expense of using explicit stage highlights. Distributing assets really guarantees a vital and supportable presence on picked stages.

Security and protection concerns have become progressively significant lately. Stages change in their ways to deal with client information and protection, and organizations should adjust their qualities to stages that focus on moral practices. Understanding the information strategies and safety efforts of every stage is significant to keeping up with entrust with your crowd.

Versatility is one more element to consider. The computerized scene develops quickly, and stages that are adaptable and can oblige arising patterns or changes in client conduct give an upper hand. Remaining informed about industry patterns and stage refreshes is fundamental to guarantee your picked stages stay successful and lined up with your objectives.

All in all, picking the right stages includes a smart examination of the interest group, objectives, content or items, rivalry, commitment inclinations, financial plan, security, and versatility. By taking into account these elements and remaining informed about industry improvements, people and organizations can settle on informed choices that add to an effective and maintainable web-based presence.

# Optimizing Video for Various Channels

Streamlining video content for different diverts is significant in the present advanced scene where various stages take special care of various crowds and inclinations. Each channel has its extraordinary determinations, prerequisites, and crowd ways of behaving, requiring an insightful way to deal with guaranteeing the most extreme reach and commitment.

**Figuring out Channel Particulars:**

Understanding the specifics of each platform is essential to begin. YouTube, for example, inclines toward high-goal recordings, with 1080p being the norm. In contrast, Instagram caters to its mobile-centric user base by favoring square or vertical videos. Realizing these particulars is the most important move towards powerful improvement.

**Ratio of Resolution to Aspect:**

One vital part of advancement is adjusting the video goal and perspective proportion for every stage. While Instagram thrives on 1:1 or 4:5 aspect ratios for square or vertical content, YouTube should use a 16:9 aspect ratio. This custom-made approach guarantees that recordings seem consistently on clients' feeds, staying away from abnormal yields or dark bars.

## Video Length and Crowd Consideration:

The length of a video is judged differently by different platforms. YouTube crowds frequently draw in with longer content, making it appropriate for top to bottom instructional exercises or narratives. Conversely, stages like TikTok blossom with short-structure content, normally going from 15 to 60 seconds. Understanding the focusing ability of every crowd is pivotal in making content that keeps watchers snared.

## Spellbinding Thumbnails:

A video's thumbnails are its first impression. Fitting them to line up with the stage's stylish and catching watchers' eye is imperative. YouTube thumbnails ought to be high-goal and obviously address the video's substance. Instagram, with its accentuation on visual allure, requires thumbnails that are connecting as well as fit consistently into clients' feeds.

## Using Inscriptions and Captions:

Taking into account the different ways individuals consume content, consolidating inscriptions or captions is a shrewd methodology. Facebook, for example, auto-plays recordings without sound, making captions fundamental for passing on the message successfully. Subtitles also help YouTube reach a wider audience and improve accessibility.

**Advancing for Versatile Review:**

Given the rising commonness of versatile clients, improving recordings for more modest screens is basic. Vertical recordings, predominant on stages like TikTok and Instagram Stories, genuinely take advantage of versatile land. Guaranteeing text and significant visuals are apparent on more modest screens improves the general client experience.

**Adapting content to the preferences of the audience:**

Every stage draws in a particular segment with unmistakable inclinations. Understanding these inclinations assists in fitting with satisfying in like manner. LinkedIn, for instance, is more business-oriented, making it a better fit for content that is professionally presented. Snapchat, on the other hand, encourages content that is more casual and authentic because of its success.

**Website design enhancement Improvement:**

Advancing video content for web crawlers isn't restricted to composed content. Findability can be improved by including relevant keywords in the titles, descriptions, and tags of videos. YouTube, being a hunt driven stage, depends vigorously on this improvement. Creating convincing and catchphrase rich titles can essentially influence a video's perceivability.

**Steady Marking Across Stages:**

While adjusting content to fit every stage's necessities, it is significant to keep a reliable brand personality. This incorporates utilizing a similar logo, variety plans, and generally speaking tasteful. A user experience that is consistent across platforms builds brand recognition.

**Commitment Procedures:**

Every stage empowers various types of commitment. Instagram relies heavily on visually engaging content that encourages users to interact through likes and comments, whereas YouTube thrives on comments, likes, and shares. Understanding the commitment elements of every stage supports making content that resounds with the crowd and ignites significant connections.

**Examination and Iterative Improvement:**

At long last, routinely examining execution measurements and client commitment is fundamental for persistent improvement. Using examination apparatuses given by stages helps in understanding what works and what doesn't. Iterative refinement in view of these experiences guarantees that future substance adjusts all the more really with the crowd's inclinations.

All in all, upgrading video content for different channels includes a complex methodology, taking into account specialized details, crowd ways of behaving, and stage elements. A custom fitted procedure that incorporates goal, viewpoint proportion, length, and commitment strategies guarantees that recordings contact a more extensive crowd as well as resound successfully with every stage's client base. Adaptability and up-to-date knowledge are still essential for successful video optimization, even as the digital landscape continues to change.

# Leveraging Social Media for Maximum Impact

Utilizing online entertainment for greatest effect is essential in the present interconnected world. Web-based entertainment stages have advanced past simple specialized instruments, turning out to be strong channels for brand advancement, data scattering, and local area building. Understanding how to bridle the capability of these stages can fundamentally upgrade your range and impact.

**1. Identify Your Goals:**
Prior to plunging into the online entertainment scene, obviously frame your objectives. Whether it's rising image mindfulness, driving site traffic, or encouraging client commitment, having clear cut targets will direct your procedure and content creation.

**2. Comprehend where Your Audience members may come from:**
Understanding your interest group is central to compelling virtual entertainment usage. Break down socioeconomics, interests, and ways of behaving to tailor your substance to resound with your crowd. Customized and significant substance is bound to catch consideration and make commitment.

### 3. Pick the Right Stages:

Not all online entertainment stages are made equivalent. Select stages that line up with your ideal interest group and business goals. For example, Instagram might be great for outwardly engaging substance, while LinkedIn could take special care of a more expert crowd. Tailor your way to deal with every stage's assets.

### 4. Steady Marking:

Keep a durable brand picture across all stages. Reliable visuals, tone, and informing fabricate memorability. A uniform brand presence encourages trust and believability among your crowd.

### 5. Quality written substance is the final deciding factor:

Create content that your audience will find valuable and shareable. This could incorporate educational articles, eye-getting visuals, or engaging recordings. A different substance procedure keeps your crowd connected with and urges them to share your substance, enhancing your scope.

### 6. Draw in with Your Crowd:

Online entertainment is definitely not a single direction road. Effectively draw in with your crowd by answering remarks, seeking clarification on some things, and partaking in conversations. Loyalty and the likelihood of your content being shared are both enhanced when there is a sense of community surrounding your brand.

### 7. Use Visual Substance:

On social media, visual content typically performs exceptionally well. Put resources into great pictures, infographics, and recordings to enamor your crowd. Stages like Instagram, Pinterest, and TikTok blossom with outwardly engaging substance.

## 8. Influence Powerhouse Showcasing:

Your reach can grow exponentially by partnering with industry influencers. Powerhouses have laid out entrust with their supporters, and a positive underwriting from them can upgrade your image's believability. Guarantee arrangement between your image values and those of the powerhouse.

## 9. Paid Promoting:

Consider designating a piece of your spending plan to pay publicizing via virtual entertainment stages. Designated promotions can arrive at explicit socioeconomics, improving the probability of arriving at likely clients. Web-based entertainment publicizing gives definite examination, empowering you to refine your system in view of execution measurements.

## 10. Screen Examination:

Routinely investigate the presentation of your web-based entertainment endeavors utilizing stage examination instruments. Comprehend what content resounds most with your crowd, the ideal posting times, and commitment measurements. Utilize this information to refine your technique and amplify influence.

## 11. Accept Changes and Obstacles:

Keep up to date with virtual entertainment patterns and difficulties. Take part in famous hashtags or challenges that line up with your image. This increments perceivability as well as grandstands your image's capacity to adjust and interface with current internet based culture.

## 12. Lay out a Posting Timetable:
In social media, consistency is essential. Lay out a posting plan that lines up with your crowd's web-based propensities. Normal and unsurprising substance keeps up with crowd interest and keeps your image top-of-mind.

## 13. Keep an eye on your rivals:
Watch out for your rivals' web-based entertainment exercises. Comprehend what functions admirably for themselves and recognize likely holes in their system that you can take advantage of. This serious investigation can give important bits of knowledge to improving your own online entertainment approach.

## 14. Support Client Created Content:
Urge your crowd to make and share content connected with your image. Client created content fills in as valid tributes as well as grows your scope as supporters share their encounters with your items or administrations.

## 15. Remain Credible:
Legitimacy assembles trust. Be authentic in your connections, concede botches when important, and exhibit the human side of your image. Validness reverberates with crowds and cultivates long haul connections.

All in all, utilizing virtual entertainment for most extreme effect requires a vital and all encompassing methodology. From characterizing targets to remaining legitimate, every component adds to building areas of strength for a powerful internet based presence. Remain versatile, dissect information consistently, and embrace the powerful idea of virtual entertainment to guarantee supported progress in the advanced scene.

# Chapter 4 Measuring Success and Key Metrics for Video Marketing

Estimating progress in video promoting is vital for improving methodologies, designating assets actually, and showing profit from venture. The outcome of a video showcasing effort goes past simple perspectives; it includes different measurements that give bits of knowledge into crowd commitment, brand effect, and transformation rates.

**View Counts:**

View counts are the most essential measurement, showing the times a video has been watched. Although high view counts may appear to indicate success, the quality of those views must be taken into consideration. Did viewers continue to watch the video after a few seconds, or did they stop? Stages like YouTube and Vimeo frequently give itemized examinations, including normal view terms.

**Commitment Rates:**

Estimating how watchers communicate with your video is critical. Commitment rates incorporate preferences, remarks, offers, and navigate rates. A high level of engagement indicates that the content resonates with the audience, leading to a deeper connection and the possibility of sharing. Breaking down remarks can likewise give important subjective bits of knowledge into crowd feelings.

**Change Measurements:**

At last, video advertising intends to drive explicit activities, for example, item buys, recruits, or downloads. Assessment of the campaign's impact on the bottom line is aided by tracking conversion metrics like click-through rates to a website, completed forms, or product sales directly attributed to the video.

**Watch Time and Maintenance:**

Past view counts, understanding how long watchers spend watching your video is significant. Dissecting watch time and crowd consistency standards gives experiences into the video's viability in holding crowd consideration. High degrees of consistency show that the substance is connected with and important all through its span.

**Metrics for Social Media:**

Metrics that are unique to each social media platform must be tracked when distributing videos. On Facebook, for instance, you can screen video finish rates, responses, and offers. Twitter provides video view counts and engagement metrics, whereas

Instagram provides insights into story views. Fitting your examination to every stage one of a kind measurements guarantees a more exact evaluation of execution.

**Brand Mindfulness and Reach:**

Evaluating brand influence includes analyzing measurements connected with brand specifics, searches, and site traffic following the video crusade. Devices like Google Examination can assist with following how video content adds to expand brand mindfulness and drive natural traffic.

**Crowd Socioeconomics:**

Understanding your crowd is vital for making designated and applicable substances. Your audience can be better understood by looking at demographic data like age, gender, location, and the device used to watch the video. Future content creation and distribution strategies can be influenced by this information.

**Profit from Speculation (return for money invested):**

Computing the return for money invested in a video showcasing effort includes looking at the expenses caused (creation, dissemination, advancement) with the income produced. This comprehensive metric establishes a direct link between the campaign's financial impact and success.

**Metrics for Email and Landing Pages:**

Assuming your video advertising system incorporates email missions or points of arrival, following measurements like open rates, navigate rates, and change rates on these stages assesses the video's viability in driving activities past the underlying perspective.

**Surveys and Comments:**
Direct input from your crowd is priceless. Carrying out reviews or assembling input through remarks can give subjective experiences into how your crowd sees the video content. This data can be utilized to refine future missions.

**Cutthroat Examination:**
Benchmarking your video execution against industry contenders can give setting to progress. Breaking down their measurements and techniques can offer significant experiences into what works in your industry and assist with recognizing regions for development.

All in all, estimating progress in video promoting includes a diverse methodology that goes past basic view counts. By looking at commitment, transformations, crowd socioeconomics, and other significant measurements, advertisers can acquire a comprehensive comprehension of a video mission's effect. Routinely breaking down and adjusting systems in light of these measurements is fundamental for remaining ahead in the powerful scene of video advertising.

# Analyzing Engagement and Conversion Rates

Breaking down commitment and transformation rates is vital for organizations looking to streamline their internet based presence and advertising systems. These measurements give significant bits of knowledge into client collaborations, assisting associations with understanding the adequacy of their endeavors in drawing in and holding clients. In this conversation, we'll dig into the meaning of commitment and change rates, techniques for examination, and procedures for development.

**Understanding Commitment and Change Rates:**

Commitment alludes to the degree of client contribution with a site, application, or promoting content. It includes different activities, like snaps, likes, remarks, and time spent on a page. An engaging user experience and content that resonates with the intended audience are both indicators of high engagement.

Transformation rates, then again, measure the level of clients who make an ideal move, like making a buy, pursuing a pamphlet, or finishing up a structure. A high transformation rate means that a critical piece of connected clients is traveling through the deals channel and finishing the expected objective.

**How Important Analysis Is:**

Breaking down commitment and transformation rates gives a far reaching comprehension of client conduct and the viability of showcasing systems. Businesses can use this data-driven strategy to make better decisions, better allocate resources, and refine their campaigns for better results.

Commitment measurements like navigate rates (CTR), skip rates, and virtual entertainment cooperations offer experiences into client inclinations and the effect of showcasing messages. By looking at these measurements, organizations can recognize high-performing content, figure out client inclinations, and design their systems likewise.

Transformation rates, frequently estimated as the proportion of changes to add up to guests, feature the outcome of a site or mission in changing over intrigued clients into clients. Businesses can improve the conversion process as a whole, optimize user journeys, and pinpoint areas for improvement by analyzing conversion data.

## Strategies for Investigation:

Google Examination and Comparative Devices:

Using examination instruments like Google Investigation gives a thorough outline of site execution. Following client connections, traffic sources, and transformation ways assists organizations with distinguishing qualities and shortcomings in their web-based presence.

## A/B Testing:

A/B testing includes making at least two renditions of a website page or promoting material and contrasting their presentation. By dissecting client conduct on various varieties, organizations can recognize components that add to higher commitment and transformation rates.

## Client Criticism and Overviews:

Direct criticism from clients through overviews or client service communications can give subjective bits of knowledge into their encounters. Understanding client feelings and tending to trouble spots can emphatically affect commitment and change rates.

**Techniques for Development:**

**Enhancing Client Experience (UX):**

A consistent and easy to understand experience is fundamental for high commitment. Further developing site route, guaranteeing quick burden times, and upgrading versatile responsiveness add to a positive client experience.

**Content Importance:**

Fitting substance to address the issues and interests of the interest group is urgent. Consistently refreshing and enhancing content in view of client criticism and inclinations can support commitment and empower changes.

**CTAs (clear calls to action):**

Very much planned and decisively positioned CTAs guide clients toward wanted activities. Guaranteeing clearness and pertinence in CTAs can fundamentally affect change rates by limiting grinding in the client venture.

**Personalization:**

Customizing content and showcasing messages in view of client conduct and inclinations makes a more individualized encounter. Personalization cultivates an association with clients, improving the probability of commitment and changes.

**Execution Observing and Iterative Changes:**

Consistently observing commitment and change measurements permits organizations to recognize patterns and examples. Executing iterative changes in view of information examination guarantees a dynamic and versatile way to deal with improvement.

Taking everything into account, the investigation of commitment and change rates is a necessary piece of any effective advanced advertising technique. By understanding client conduct, upgrading client experience, and consistently refining content and missions, organizations can improve their internet based presence and drive significant outcomes. The mix of quantitative examination and subjective bits of knowledge shapes a strong starting point for vital direction and supports progress in the unique computerized scene.

# Chapter 5 Case Studies and Successful Video Marketing Campaigns

Case studies are a great way to learn about the methods and strategies that businesses use to succeed in a variety of areas of their operations. With regards to video showcasing, looking at fruitful missions through contextual investigations can offer a guide for different organizations expecting to upgrade their computerized presence. In this investigation, we will examine a number of notable video marketing campaigns and the most important factors that contributed to their success.

One excellent contextual analysis is the "Pigeon Genuine Magnificence Portrayals" crusade. Sent off by Bird in 2013, this mission was meant to challenge the cultural view of magnificence. The video highlighted a FBI-prepared scientific craftsman who portrayed ladies in view of their self-portraits and afterward again founded on the depictions of outsiders. The strong disclosure was that the representations made according to outsiders' viewpoints were seriously complimenting, featuring the unforgiving self-analysis numerous ladies force on themselves.

The content of the Dove Real Beauty Sketches campaign resonated with people on an emotional level and was in line with the overall Dove brand message of encouraging self-esteem and real beauty. Dove not only garnered widespread attention but also strengthened its brand identity by addressing a universal problem, establishing a connection with its intended audience.

Another convincing model is the "Offer a Coke" crusade by Coca-Cola. This mission customized the item by supplanting the Coca-Cola logo on its containers with well known names, empowering individuals to find and impart a Coke to loved ones. The promoting group made it a stride further by consolidating client created content, empowering customers to share photographs with their customized Coke bottles via virtual entertainment.

The "Share a Coke" campaign's innovative approach to personalization and social media integration are to blame for its success. Coca-Cola increased brand engagement and created a sense of connection among its customers by leveraging the power of user-generated content and encouraging social sharing.

The "The Man Your Man Could Smell Like" campaign by Old Spice is yet another case study that merits investigation. Sent off in 2010, this viral mission highlighted a charming representative conveying clever and critical discourses while exhibiting different Old Flavor items. The cunning utilization of humor and the eccentric way to deal with publicizing made the mission hang out in a packed market.

Old Zest's prosperity with this mission lies in its capacity to catch watchers' consideration with engaging substance and make a vital brand persona. The mission's effect was additionally intensified by its intelligent component, as Old Flavor answered constant remarks and inquiries via virtual entertainment with customized video reactions. This not only kept the audience interested, but it also showed how responsive the brand is and how willing it is to connect directly with customers.

The success of video marketing campaigns is largely attributed to the common factors highlighted in these case studies. The power of narrative is the most important factor. Every one of these missions recounted a convincing story that reverberated with the main interest group, whether it was testing magnificent norms, advancing unique interactions, or conveying humor surprisingly.

Besides, close to home allure assumed a huge part in these missions. By addressing issues related to self-esteem, Dove's Real Beauty Sketches, Coca-Cola's Share a Coke, and Old Spice's humorous approach all elicited positive emotions. Effective video promotion frequently goes past items, taking advantage of the close to home perspectives that establish a long term connection with watchers.

Another important aspect is the incorporation of social media. Utilizing social media platforms can significantly expand a video marketing campaign's reach and impact in the digital age. Coca-Cola's Portion a Coke crusade effectively empowered social sharing, while Old Zest's intelligent reactions via web-based entertainment made a two-way discussion with the crowd. This lifts commitment as well as permits brands to interface with customers progressively.

Personalization also emerged as a significant theme in these successful campaigns. Coca-Cola's customized containers and Old Flavor's customized video reactions showed a comprehension of the singular purchaser. Personalization makes a feeling of eliteness and causes shoppers to feel seen and esteemed, encouraging a more grounded association with the brand.

In addition, these case studies emphasize the significance of creativity and adaptability. Dove tested customary magnificence principles, Coca-Cola reexamined its bundling, and Old Flavor embraced unpredictable humor. Fruitful video promotion requires a readiness to break new ground, face challenges, and remain sensitive to changing shopper inclinations.

businesses looking to improve their digital marketing efforts can benefit greatly from case studies of successful video marketing campaigns. The Pigeon Genuine Magnificence Portrayals, Offer a Coke, and The Man Your Man Could Smell Like missions grandstand the force of narrating, close to home allure, online entertainment joining, personalization, and innovativeness. Businesses can improve their video marketing strategies and produce compelling content that resonates with their target audience by studying these examples. This will ultimately increase brand awareness, engagement, and loyalty.

# Lessons Learned from Notable Examples

Businesses can now effectively connect with their audience and increase engagement with video marketing. Gaining from prominent models can give significant bits of knowledge into what works and what doesn't in this powerful field.

## 1. Narrating is Critical

Quite possibly the most significant example comes from brands like Nike and Apple, who have become amazing at narrating. Recordings that recount a convincing story enthrall watchers and make an enduring impression. The story ought to reverberate with the crowd, bringing out feelings that produce an association with the brand.

## 2. Validness Constructs Trust

Shoppers long for realness, and video is a superb mechanism for displaying it. Brands like Pigeon have effectively utilized valid narrating to construct trust. Straightforward and real happy encourages an association with the crowd, laying out believability and devotion.

## 3. Short and Smart for Consideration

In the period of limited ability to focus, curtness is vital. Take motivation from stages like TikTok and Instagram, where brief recordings snatch consideration rapidly. Creating content that effectively conveys the message keeps viewers engaged throughout the video.

## 4. Portable Improvement Matters

Given the predominance of cell phones, improving recordings for versatile review is an unquestionable necessity. Brands like BuzzFeed's Delectable have succeeded in making dynamic substance, perceiving the significance of a consistent survey insight on cell phones. Vertical recordings and clear visuals improve the portable survey insight.

## 5. Intuitiveness Improves Commitment

Intuitive recordings can fundamentally support commitment. Bandersnatch on Netflix is a great example of how interactive content can completely immerse viewers. The inclusion of polls, clickable elements, or "choose-your-own-adventure" scenarios keeps viewers engaged and enhances the experience.

## 6. Consistency Establishes Brand Identity

It is essential for recognition to maintain a consistent brand image across videos. This is shown by the high-adrenaline content of Red Bull. Consistency in style, tone, and informing supports brand character, making it effectively conspicuous and building up brand values.

## 7. Website design enhancement Streamlining for Perceivability

Upgrading recordings for web search tools is frequently ignored however can significantly influence perceivability. YouTube is the second-biggest web crawler internationally, accentuating the requirement for appropriate watchwords, portrayals, and labels. Executing Search engine optimization best practices guarantees that your recordings are discoverable by a more extensive crowd.

## 8. Embrace Patterns however Remain Valid

While riding on the latest things can support perceivability, remaining consistent with your brand is fundamental. Old Flavor's "The Man Your Man Could Smell Like" crusade flawlessly coordinated humor and viral advertising. Remaining bona fide to your image while embracing patterns guarantees that your substance stays pertinent and resounds with your ideal interest group.

**9. Use Tributes and Client produced Content**

Genuine encounters shared through tributes and client produced content can propel. GoPro, for instance, built its brand on user-generated content that showcased the community's adventures. Integrating tributes and client content adds genuineness and energizes crowd support.

**10. Measure and Break down Execution**

Information driven direction is vital in video promotion. Stages like Google Examination and online entertainment experiences give significant measurements. Understanding what works by analyzing performance metrics on a regular basis makes it possible to modify and enhance subsequent campaigns.

**11. Develop Serious areas of strength for a to-Activity (CTA)**

Each video ought to direct the watcher on what to do straightaway. A solid CTA prompts activity, whether it's meeting a site, buying in, or making a buy. Blendtec's "Will It Mix?" series engaged as well as incorporated an unmistakable CTA, driving item deals.

**12. Localization with a Global Impact**

Are you thinking about a global audience? Limitation is critical. Airbnb actually fits its video content to various business sectors, guaranteeing social pertinence. Resonance with a wide range of audiences is enhanced by adapting videos to local languages and customs.

### 13. Adjust to Arising Advances

It is significant to Remain in front of mechanical progressions. Virtual and expanded the truth are turning out to be more available, giving open doors to vivid video encounters. Brands like IKEA have embraced AR to permit clients to envision furniture in their homes prior to buying.

### 14. Emergency The board through Straightforwardness

In the midst of an emergency, straightforward correspondence is principal. Johnson and Johnson's reaction to the Tylenol harming emergency during the 1980s displayed the significance of resolving issues transparently. Video can be a useful asset for the emergency board, showing responsibility and obligation to the goal.

All in all, the scene of video advertising is constantly advancing, and gaining from fruitful models is significant. Businesses can create compelling video content that resonates with their audience, builds trust, and drives meaningful engagement by mastering storytelling, embracing authenticity, optimizing for mobile, and remaining abreast of trends and technologies.

# Chapter 6
# Tools and Resources

Because it makes use of the power of images to effectively engage audiences and convey messages, video marketing has emerged as an essential component of contemporary digital strategies. To explore the unique scene of video content creation and advancement, organizations and makers depend on a plenty of devices and assets. These incorporate many angles, from video creation and altering to investigation and circulation.

**Video Creation Devices:**

**Adobe Debut Expert:**

Generally utilized by experts, this video altering programming offers progressed highlights for consistent video creation, including multi-camera altering and vigorous variety amendment instruments.

**Finished product Master X:**

A favored decision for Macintosh clients, Finished product Master X gives an easy to understand interface and strong altering capacities, making it ideal for the two novices and experienced video editors.

**Camtasia:**

Known for its effortlessness, Camtasia is a phenomenal device for screen recording and video altering. It's especially valuable for making instructional exercise recordings and instructive substance.

**Visual depiction and Activity Devices:**

**Adobe Eventual outcomes:**

This device is basic for adding enhancements and liveliness to recordings, improving visual allure and commitment.

**Canva:**

While essentially a visual communication device, Canva likewise offers video altering capacities, permitting clients to make outwardly engaging video satisfied easily.

**Examination and Execution Following:**

**Google Examination:**

Past sites, Google Examination can be incorporated with video stages, giving bits of knowledge into watcher conduct, commitment measurements, and segment data.

**Wistia:**

In addition to hosting videos, this platform offers analytics on viewer engagement, assisting businesses in comprehending how audiences interact with their content.

**Resources for Distribution and Promotion:**

**YouTube:**

The biggest video-sharing stage worldwide, YouTube is a foundation for video promotion. Its tremendous client base and search usefulness make it a fundamental channel for content appropriation.

**Vimeo:**

Known for its top notch video playback, Vimeo is a favored stage for creatives holding back nothing proficient and imaginative touch in their substance.

**Platforms for social media:**

Facebook, Instagram, and Twitter: These stages offer video-sharing capacities, and their broad client bases make them important channels for advancing video content.

**Arising Innovations:**

**Computer generated Reality (VR) and Expanded Reality (AR):**

As these advances develop, coordinating them into video promoting can give vivid and drawing encounters, however their boundless reception is still in its beginning phases.

**Video Showcasing Procedure:**

Effective video promotion goes past apparatuses and stages.Fostering a complete strategy is fundamental.This includes characterizing main interest groups, setting clear targets, making convincing substance, and persistently examining execution measurements to refine methodologies after some time.

All in all, the apparatuses and assets accessible for video showcasing are assorted and always advancing. Organizations and content makers should keep up to date with industry patterns and influence the right mix of devices to make, advance, and examine video content really in a serious computerized scene.

# Video Editing Software

Video altering programming assumes an urgent part in the after creation process, changing crude film into cleaned, drawing in satisfaction. With the persistent development of innovation, a plenty of video altering instruments are accessible, taking care of different expertise levels and prerequisites. The features, ease of use, and hardware compatibility of a video editing software are all important considerations for both amateur and professional filmmakers.

One of the trailblazers in the video altering scene is Adobe Debut Ace. Known for its strong and flexible highlights, Debut Star is generally utilized in the film and broadcast business. Its timetable based interface takes into consideration exact altering, and it consistently incorporates with other Adobe Innovative Cloud applications, working with a smooth work process. Debut Genius offers progressed variety evaluating instruments, sound altering capacities, and backing for an extensive variety of document designs. Compatibility with the most recent camera technologies and industry standards is ensured by the software's regular updates.

On the other hand, iMovie is a popular choice for people who want a more straightforward and easy-to-use option. Created by Macintosh, iMovie is pre-introduced on Macintosh PCs and is accessible as a free download for iOS gadgets. iMovie's natural point of interaction makes it open to novices, while offering fundamental elements like cutting, managing, and adding advances. Albeit not as component rich as some expert programming, iMovie is an amazing beginning stage for people wandering into video altering interestingly.

For Windows clients, Windows Film Creator has been a staple for fundamental video altering needs. Nonetheless, starting around my last information update in January 2022, Microsoft had authoritatively stopped Film Producer. Nowadays, alternatives like Shotcut and DaVinci Resolve are frequently used by Windows users. Shotcut is an open-source, cross-stage video altering programming that gives a great many elements, including support for different video designs and codecs. DaVinci Resolve, at first known for its variety reviewing capacities, has developed into an extensive after creation arrangement. Visual effects, audio post-production, advanced editing tools, and even 3D editing are all part of it.

The rise of cloud-based video editing solutions is a noteworthy development of recent years. One such model is WeVideo, an electronic stage that permits clients to alter recordings cooperatively on the web. Because the editing takes place on remote servers, this method does not necessitate powerful hardware. WeVideo is reasonable for the two fledgling and more experienced editors, offering a scope of elements, changes, and a library of stock media.

For experts in the field of enhanced visualizations and 3D movement, Autodesk's Maya and Blackmagic Combination are vital apparatuses. Maya, initially intended for 3D movement, has extended its capacities to incorporate video altering highlights. It is broadly utilized in the making of enlivened films and enhanced visualizations for blockbuster motion pictures. DaVinci Resolve Studio's Blackmagic Fusion is a compositing and visual effects specialist. Its hub based interface gives an adaptable and strong method for making unpredictable enhanced visualizations groupings.

Cell phones have additionally become amazing assets for video altering, because of uses like LumaFusion for iOS. LumaFusion offers a thorough arrangement of altering highlights, including multi-track altering, high level variety revision, and backing for high-goal video. It's easy to understand interface makes it a #1 among versatile movie producers and vloggers who need to alter in a hurry.

While examining video altering programming, the significance of proficient work processes couldn't possibly be more significant. Apple Finished product Master X is eminent for its improved work process on Macintosh frameworks. Its attractive course of events takes into consideration a liquid and dynamic altering experience, making it more straightforward for editors to try different things with various cuts and game plans. Finished product Genius X additionally exploits Apple's Metal system, expanding equipment speed increase for smoother playback and delivering.

For the individuals who favor open-source arrangements, Lightworks sticks out. Accessible for Windows, Linux, and macOS, Lightworks offers a free rendition with strong altering highlights. It has been utilized in the altering of component films like "The Wolf of Money Road." The product upholds an extensive variety of record configurations and goals, settling on it a flexible decision for different undertakings.

All in all, the universe of video altering programming is assorted, taking special care of a wide range of clients with various necessities and expertise levels. Whether you're a hopeful substance maker or a carefully prepared producer, the decision of programming relies upon your particular prerequisites, financial plan limitations, and the intricacy of the tasks you embrace. From proficient grade instruments like Adobe Debut Expert and DaVinci Resolve to easy to understand choices like iMovie and WeVideo, the wealth of decisions guarantees that there's a video altering answer for everybody. As innovation keeps on propelling, we can expect considerably more inventive elements and natural points of interaction to further improve the video altering experience.

# Analytics and Monitoring Tools

Examination and observing devices assume a vital part in the progress of video promoting procedures. In a period overwhelmed by advanced content, organizations influence recordings to connect with crowds and pass on their messages actually. In any case, the simple creation and conveyance of recordings are adequately not; Optimizing marketing efforts requires a thorough understanding of how viewers interact with these videos. This is where investigation and observing instruments become possibly the most important factor.

**Grasping Client Conduct:**
Analytics tools give you a lot of useful information about how users act. They keep track of metrics like the number of views, the amount of time watched, and the percentage of people who engaged, which helps marketers figure out which videos are popular with their target

audience. Businesses can find patterns and preferences by looking at these metrics, which allows them to tailor future content to meet the expectations of their audience.

**Transformation Following:**

Compelling video showcasing reaches out past perspectives; it's tied in with changing over watchers into clients. Examination apparatuses permit organizations to follow transformation rates, giving bits of knowledge into how well their recordings are driving wanted activities, for example, recruits, buys, or structure entries. This information is instrumental in refining, promoting techniques and advancing the change pipe.

**Segmenting an Audience:**

Not all crowds are similar, and examination instruments assist organizations with sectioning their watchers in light of socio economics, area, and survey gadgets. By allowing for targeted content creation, this segmentation ensures that videos appeal to specific audience segments. Businesses can increase customer engagement and cultivate a more devoted following by creating content that is tailored to various demographics.

**Continuous Checking:**

Video performance can be monitored in real time with monitoring tools. This permits advertisers to respond immediately to patterns or issues, upgrading their techniques on the fly. Constant checking is particularly basic during live occasions or item dispatches, where quick changes can fundamentally affect the general progress of the mission.

**Web-based Entertainment Joining:**
Numerous video advertising efforts are disseminated across different online entertainment stages. Investigation instruments frequently incorporate these stages, giving a united perspective on video execution across channels. Marketers can adjust their strategy based on the impact of their videos on various platforms thanks to this integration.

**Website design enhancement Advancement:**
Examination devices can likewise help with enhancing recordings for web search tools. By examining watchwords, client commitment, and other important measurements, organizations can upgrade the discoverability of their recordings. This Website design enhancement streamlining guarantees that recordings rank higher in query items, expanding perceivability and drawing in a bigger crowd.

**The A/B Test:**
Powerful video advertising requires consistent trial and error. Analytics tools make A/B testing easier by letting marketers compare how different versions of a video perform. By testing factors like thumbnails, titles, or video lengths, organizations can refine their substance system in light of what reverberates best with their crowd.

**Execution Benchmarking:**
To check the outcome of video advertising endeavors, organizations need to benchmark their exhibition against industry principles. Marketers can use benchmarking data provided by analytics tools to compare their metrics to industry averages. This

benchmarking helps put forth reasonable objectives and gives an unmistakable comprehension of where enhancements can be made.

**Compliance with Data Security and Privacy:**

Analytics tools must adhere to regulations and safeguard user data in this day and age when privacy and security of data are increasingly important concerns. Marketers ought to select tools that place an emphasis on safety and ensure compliance with relevant privacy laws. This protections client data as well as constructs entrust with the crowd.

In the powerful scene of video promoting, examination and observing devices are irreplaceable for progress. They enable organizations to figure out their crowd, advance substance, and boost the effect of their video crusades. From following client conduct to continuous checking and Website design enhancement streamlining, these devices give a thorough tool compartment to advertisers endeavoring to remain ahead in the serious universe of computerized showcasing. By utilizing the experiences given by examination apparatuses, organizations can make more designated, connecting with, and compelling video content, at last driving progress in their showcasing tries.

# Tips for Budget-Friendly Production

Making a spending plan cordial video showcasing effort requires an essential way to deal with guarantee cost-viability without compromising quality. Here are key tips to hold your creation costs under control:

**Effective Content Planning:**

Create a comprehensive storyboard or script outline before pressing the record button. This pre-creation arranging limits retakes and altering time, diminishing generally creation costs. Obviously characterize your message, ideal interest group, and wanted results to smooth out the shooting system.

**Put resources into Quality Gear:**

While it could appear to be illogical for spending plan cordial creation, it is vital to put resources into fair hardware. Section level DSLR cameras and cell phones frequently give top notch video for a portion of the expense of expert camcorders. Great lighting hardware can likewise altogether improve the visual allure of your recordings.

**Do-It-Yourself          Lighting Arrangements:**

Legitimate lighting is fundamental for quality video creation. Investigate cost-effective DIY solutions rather than spending a lot of money on professional lighting kits. Use regular light, reasonable Drove lights, or even family lights decisively positioned to accomplish the ideal lighting impacts. Trying different things with various arrangements can yield proficient looking outcomes without burning through every last dollar.

**Upgrade Sound on a Careful spending plan:**

Unfortunate sound quality can cheapen even the most outwardly engaging video. Put resources into a financial plan accommodating the outer mouthpiece to further develop sound catch. On the other hand, investigate reasonable after creation sound improvement devices to clean your sound quality during altering.

**Pick the Right Area:**

Time and money can be saved by picking a good shooting location. Pick settings that normally supplement your message and lessen the requirement for intricate set plans. Public spaces, sufficiently bright rooms, or even open air conditions can act as financially savvy backgrounds.

**Use Free or Reasonable Altering Programming:**

There are various free or minimal expense video altering devices accessible that offer strong elements. Programming like Shotcut, Lightworks, or DaVinci Resolve gives proficient grade altering abilities without the strong sticker price. Focus intensely on learning the intricate details of these instruments to boost their true capacity.

**Excel at Do-It-Yourself Illustrations:**

Abstain from reevaluating visual computerization by figuring out how to make straightforward designs and overlays yourself. Online stages like Canva or Adobe Flash proposition easy to understand connection points and layouts for making eye-getting visuals. For every video project, this skill can help you save money on hiring a designer.

**Embrace Client Created Content:**

Urge your crowd to contribute content, whether it's tributes, surveys, or inventive translations connected with your item or administration. Client created content diminishes creation costs as well as cultivates a feeling of local area around your image.

**Investigate Reasonable Ability Choices:**

On the off chance that your video requires ability before the camera, think about neighborhood entertainers or even colleagues. Recruiting nearby ability is much of the time more expensive than acquiring experts, and it can add legitimacy to your recordings.

**Boost Virtual Entertainment Stages:**

Influence the force of online entertainment stages for dissemination. Make more limited, connecting with recordings that are custom fitted to every stage's particulars. This not only ensures that your content is optimized for each channel, increasing its impact, but also reaches a larger audience.

**Reuse Content:**

Capitalize on your video creation by reusing content across different stages and organizations. Transform longer recordings into more limited cuts, make GIFs, or remove sound for digital broadcasts. This approach augments the worth of your underlying speculation.

**Arrange and Trade Administrations:**

While working with consultants or specialist co-ops, make sure to rate or investigate deal plans. Numerous experts are available to adapt plans, particularly on the off chance that you can give a help or item as a trade off.

**Screen Patterns and Remain Adaptable:**

Watch out for industry drifts and adjust your substance system likewise. Remaining on top of things permits you to deliver applicable and drawing in happiness without putting resources into expensive last-minute changes.

**DIY Animated Videos:**

Energized components can upgrade your recordings without the requirement for costly programming or experts. Investigate Do-It-Yourself liveliness devices like Powtoon, Vyond, or even free options like Blender for further developed clients.

**Work with influential people:**

Produce associations with powerhouses or content makers who line up with your image. Powerhouse coordinated efforts can give admittance to a more extensive crowd while frequently being more savvy than customary publicizing strategies.

By executing these financial plan accommodating tips, you can make convincing video showcasing efforts that really convey your message without burning through every last cent. Key preparation, creative arrangements, and an eagerness to investigate new roads will enable you to accomplish noteworthy outcomes inside your monetary limitations.

# Chapter 7
# Future
# Trends in

# Video Marketing

There are a number of trends influencing the future of video marketing, which is undergoing rapid change. As innovation advances and shopper inclinations shift, organizations need to keep up to date with these improvements to make convincing and compelling video content. From expanded reality (AR) reconciliation to customized encounters, here are a few vital future patterns in video showcasing.

**1. Intelligent Video Content:**

Intuitive recordings are building up forward momentum as they offer a two-way correspondence channel. Watchers can draw in with the substance by deciding or connecting with components inside the video. This vivid experience catches consideration as well as gives a more customized venture. Intuitive shoppable recordings, for example, empower clients to tap on things inside the video and make buys straightforwardly.

**2. Integration of Augmented Reality (AR):**

AR is progressively turning into a piece of the video showcasing scene. Brands are using AR to give intuitive and drawing encounters. This could be anything from fashion brands' virtual try-on experiences to augmented reality product demonstrations. The capacity to mix the virtual and genuine universes upgrades the general watcher experience, making it more significant and shareable.

## 3. Personalization and simulated intelligence driven Content:

The fate of video promoting lies in conveying customized content to individual watchers. Man-made brainpower (man-made intelligence) is assuming a vital part in dissecting client information to make customized video proposals. Whether it's customized item ideas or content in view of client inclinations, artificial intelligence calculations are making recordings more pertinent to the crowd, consequently expanding commitment and change rates.

## 4. Short-structure and Vertical Recordings:

Short-structure recordings, promoted by stages like TikTok and Instagram Reels, are acquiring conspicuousness. These reduced down recordings take care of the diminishing focusing ability of current crowds. Also, the ascent of vertical video designs is affected by the commonness of cell phones. Brands are adjusting their video promoting systems to fit these arrangements, guaranteeing content is effectively consumable on cell phones.

## 5. Live Streaming and Constant Commitment:

Live Streaming has turned into an integral asset for brands to interface with their crowd continuously. Whether it's in the background looks, item dispatches, or back and forth discussions, livestreams make a feeling of quickness and genuineness. Through comments and responses, viewers can participate and develop a personal connection to the brand.

**6. Narrating and Validness:**

Customers are progressively attracted to legitimate stories that resound with their qualities. Video marketing is moving away from product features and toward storytelling. Brands are zeroing in on conveying their central goal, values, and the human side of their activities. Authenticity increases engagement and customer loyalty by establishing trust and emotional connections with the audience.

**7. 360-Degree Recordings and Augmented Reality (VR):**

360-degree recordings and VR give a vivid encounter, permitting watchers to investigate a virtual climate. This is especially successful in areas like land, the travel industry, and occasions. By moving watchers to various areas or occasions, brands can make vital and significant encounters that have an enduring effect.

**8. Content created by users (UGC):**

Client produced content keeps on being an important resource in video showcasing. Brands urge their clients to make content, whether it's tributes, surveys, or innovative translations of their items. UGC adds credibility, and by exhibiting client encounters, brands can construct a feeling of local area and trust.

**9. Web-based Entertainment Predominance:**

Online entertainment stages stay key to video advertising procedures. The development of stages like TikTok, Instagram, and YouTube underscores the significance of fitting substance for each channel. Brands are making explicit substance to boost reach and commitment.

**10. Compliance and Data Privacy:**

With expanding worries about information security, brands need to guarantee their video showcasing techniques conform to guidelines. Respect for user preferences and transparency regarding data usage are crucial. Finding some kind of harmony between customized content and regarding protection will be really difficult for advertisers before very long.

All in all, the eventual fate of video showcasing is dynamic and loaded up with energizing prospects. Organizations that embrace arising patterns and advances will be better situated to spellbind their crowd and remain ahead in the always developing computerized scene. The future promises a more engaging and immersive video marketing experience for brands and consumers alike through the integration of augmented reality and virtual reality as well as interactive and personalized content.

# Emerging Technologies

Arising advancements are reforming the scene of video showcasing, offering imaginative ways for organizations to interface with their crowds and make convincing substance. As we explore through the computerized age, a few patterns and progressions are molding the eventual fate of video promoting.

**1.** **Computer generated Reality (VR) and Expanded Reality (AR):**

VR and AR innovations are changing the manner in which brands draw in with buyers. In video showcasing, VR drenches clients in a reenacted climate, giving a novel and important experience. AR, then again, overlays computerized components on this present reality, improving the watcher's discernment. With the help of these technologies, marketers can develop interactive and individualized campaigns that encourage a greater level of engagement.

**2.** **Videos in 360-Degrees:**

By allowing viewers to interact with the content from a variety of perspectives, 360-degree videos create an immersive experience for the viewer. This innovation empowers advertisers to move crowds to new conditions, whether it's a virtual visit through a property, an in the background take a gander at an item, or an intuitive narrating experience. This degree of commitment can fundamentally improve brand review and watcher maintenance.

**3.** **Computerized reasoning (man-made intelligence):**

Computer based intelligence is a distinct advantage in video promoting, giving capacities like customized content suggestions, robotized video creation, and progressed examination. Artificial intelligence calculations break down client conduct and inclinations, permitting advertisers to fit their substance to explicit crowds. This degree of personalization upgrades the general client experience and expands the adequacy of video promoting efforts.

**4. ** Intuitive Recordings:

Intelligent recordings go past conventional direct narrating by permitting watchers to partake in the substance effectively. Watchers can simply decide, investigate various storylines, or snap on intelligent components inside the video. This innovation keeps watchers connected as well as gives significant information on client inclinations, assisting advertisers with refining their methodologies for improved results.

**5. ** Live Streaming:

Live streaming has turned into an incredible asset for brands to associate with their crowds progressively. Businesses are able to broadcast events, product launches, and behind-the-scenes content thanks to platforms like Facebook Live, Instagram Live, and YouTube Live. The quickness and genuineness of live web based can encourage a more grounded association among brands and purchasers, making a feeling of local area and commitment.

**6. ** Shoppable Recordings:

Shoppable recordings consistently incorporate internet business into the review insight. The video transforms into a virtual storefront when viewers can directly purchase items by clicking on them. This smoothed out shopping experience upgrades the client venture as well as gives an extra income transfer to organizations utilizing video promoting.

**7. ** Customized Video Promoting:

Personalization is key in the present promoting scene, and video is no special case. With the assistance of information examination and computer based intelligence, advertisers can make profoundly customized video content custom-made to individual inclinations and ways of behaving. Customized recordings are bound to catch the watcher's consideration and impact them on a more profound level, eventually driving change rates.

**8. ** Voice Inquiry Streamlining:

As voice-actuated gadgets become more predominant, upgrading video content for voice search is urgent. Advertisers need to consider the conversational idea of voice look and adjust their video procedures in a like manner. To ensure visibility in voice search results, this includes using natural language in video scripts and including relevant keywords.

All in all, arising advances are reshaping the scene of video advertising, offering new roads for imagination, commitment, and customized correspondence. In the ever-changing digital landscape, businesses that embrace these advancements will be better positioned to connect with their target audiences, increase brand awareness, and ultimately achieve their marketing objectives.

# Shifting Consumer Behaviors

Moving buyer ways of behaving in video showcasing have turned into a point of convergence for organizations expecting to remain significant in a consistently developing computerized scene. The ascent of innovation and changing inclinations have essentially modified the manner in which people draw in with video content, provoking advertisers to adjust their techniques to measure up to these new assumptions.

The rise in mobile video consumption is one significant shift. With the expansion of cell phones, shoppers presently have the ability to get to video content whenever, anyplace. This has prompted a huge expansion in portable video seeing, impacting advertisers to streamline their substance for more modest screens and more limited capacities to focus. Thus, snackable substance, portrayed by brief and connecting with recordings, has turned into a well known decision for brands hoping to catch the consideration of in a hurry shoppers.

Besides, the inclination for validness has reshaped customer assumptions. Conventional, cleaned commercials are progressively being eclipsed by crude and certifiable substances. Customers are attracted to recordings that vibe valid, appealing, and less organized. This has led to client produced content, powerhouse joint efforts, and in the background glimpses, permitting brands to associate with their crowd on a more private level.

The development of web-based entertainment stages has likewise assumed a urgent part in forming buyer ways of behaving. Short-structure video content, typified by stages like TikTok, has acquired monstrous ubiquity. Marketers are making use of these platforms to produce content that is entertaining, engaging, and in line with the platform's distinctive style. The test lies in creating content that fits the stage as well as reverberates with the particular socioeconomics and social subtleties of its client base.

Notwithstanding virtual entertainment, the flood in live video utilization has adjusted the advertising scene. Live streaming creates a sense of urgency and immediacy by allowing for interaction in real time. Customers can participate in product launches, Q&A sessions, and behind-the-scenes glimpses with brands by using live video. This dynamic and intuitive methodology improves commitment and develops a local area around the brand.

Moreover, the interest for customized encounters has prompted the combination of man-made consciousness (man-made intelligence) in video promoting. Simulated intelligence calculations examine client information to convey customized content, making a more customized and pertinent review insight. Personalization goes past tending to buyers by their names; it includes grasping their inclinations, ways of behaving, and interests to organize content that reverberates on a more profound level.

Customer mindfulness and worry for maintainability have likewise impacted video promoting techniques. Consumers are increasingly placing a premium on corporate responsibility, ethical sourcing, and eco-friendly practices. Brands are integrating these qualities into their video content, displaying their obligation to social and natural causes. The conscious consumer responds well to videos that highlight community initiatives, transparent supply chains, and sustainable practices.

The developing significance of inclusivity can't be disregarded. Customers are progressively esteeming variety and portrayal in the substance they consume. Video promoting efforts that embrace variety, inclusivity, and social responsiveness reverberate with a more extensive crowd as well as consider emphatically the brand's picture. Brands are perceiving the meaning of reflecting different points of view in their narrating to associate with a worldwide and various buyer base.

Fleeting substance, portrayed by its brief nature, has gotten some forward movement, particularly on stages like Instagram and Snapchat. Advertisers are utilizing the anxiety toward passing up a major opportunity (FOMO) by making time-delicate and select substance. This approach energizes prompt commitment and urges customers to remain tuned for the most recent updates, advancements, or declarations.

shifting consumer habits are driving a significant shift in the landscape of video marketing. Among the industry's most important trends are mobile video consumption, authenticity, social media dynamics, live streaming, personalization through AI, sustainability, inclusivity, and ephemeral content. Fruitful advertisers are the individuals who perceive these movements, adjust their procedures in like manner, and make content that catches consideration as well as fabricates significant associations with the always developing purchaser base.

# CONCLUSION

## Key Strategies and Ongoing Evolution of Video Marketing

Video promoting has without a doubt turned into a critical component in the contemporary computerized scene, and its development throughout the long term has been set apart by powerful methodologies that take care of changing buyer conduct and mechanical headways. All in all, an extensive comprehension of key systems and the continuous development of video showcasing is urgent for organizations planning to flourish in this unique space. One of the major methodologies that have endured over the extreme long haul is the accentuation on narrating. Compelling video advertising goes past simple item grandstands; it tries to draw in and interface with the crowd on a more profound level. By winding around convincing accounts, brands can make a profound reverberation that cultivates brand dependability and improves the general effect of their video content. As we push ahead, this methodology is probably going to stay focal, stressing the significance of human association in a computerized time.

Moreover, the rising predominance of cell phones has reshaped video utilization propensities. Short-structure recordings, exemplified by stages like TikTok, have acquired huge fame, pushing advertisers to adjust their substance techniques. The outcome of these stages highlights the requirement for succinct, outwardly engaging recordings that catch consideration quickly. In the continuous advancement of video advertising, organizations should keep on refining their narrating methods to fit the more limited focusing ability of the present crowds.

Live streaming has arisen as a useful asset in video showcasing, furnishing an ongoing association with shoppers. Live videos' authenticity and immediateness create a sense of urgency and exclusivity, which encourages engagement. Live streaming has been used by brands to show behind-the-scenes footage, product launches, and interactive Q&A sessions. This system encourages a feeling of local area as well as lines up with the contemporary customer's longing for straightforward and genuine brand cooperations.

Personalization is another key system that has acquired noticeable quality lately. With the abundance of information accessible, advertisers can fit their video content to explicit socioeconomics, interests, and, surprisingly, individual inclinations. This improves the watcher's insight as well as improves the probability of change. The continuous development of video advertising will probably see an expanded spotlight on utilizing information investigation and man-made consciousness to convey exceptionally customized content at scale.

The incorporation of expanded reality (AR) and augmented reality (VR) innovations is ready to reclassify the video advertising scene. AR permits purchasers to connect with this present reality upgraded by computerized components, while VR submerges them in a totally virtual climate. The two innovations offer one of a kind open doors for brands to make vivid and vital encounters. As these advances become more available, organizations ought to investigate inventive ways of integrating AR and VR into their video promoting methodologies to remain on the ball.

The democratization of video creation has likewise been a sign of the developing video promoting scene. Online entertainment stages have engaged people and more modest organizations to make and share video content without the requirement for broad assets. Client produced content, when decisively tackled, can enhance a brand's span and validness. As video creation apparatuses become more easy to understand and open, organizations ought to effectively urge their crowd to add to the brand story.

Video content continues to be an important part of search engine optimization (SEO). Google's calculations progressively focus on video content, perceiving its prominence and viability. As a result, businesses should improve the discoverability of their video content by optimizing it with relevant keywords, compelling titles, and comprehensive descriptions. Video marketing is likely to become even more integrated into broader SEO strategies as it continues to evolve, affecting digital visibility as a whole.

Social obligation and supportability have become basic parts of present day brand character. Video promoting gives a strong stage to organizations to convey their obligation to social causes and natural drives. Brands that are in line with their values are actively sought after by consumers, particularly younger demographics. Socially conscious customers may be more likely to be loyal to a brand if video content highlights its efforts in corporate social responsibility.

Taking everything into account, the scene of video showcasing is dynamic, and effective techniques should consistently adjust to arising patterns. The center standards of narrating, crowd commitment, and credibility stay immortal, yet the apparatuses and advances available to us are continually developing. Organizations that embrace the continuous development of video showcasing, consolidating arising advancements, focusing on personalization, and remaining receptive to moving buyer ways of behaving, are ready to make due as well as flourish in the steadily changing computerized scene. As we look forward, the cooperative energy of imagination, innovation, and purchaser driven approaches will shape the eventual fate of video promoting, making it a basic part of a vigorous computerized showcasing procedure.

# DEAR READER

Your thoughts matter to us! if the book brought a smile or moment of respite, please Consider Sharing your experience through a review.

your feedback is invaluable in making our book even more enjoyable for following.We hope this message finds you well and enjoying your literary adventures! At we value the opinions of our readers, and we would love to hear your thoughts on **[VIDEO MARKETING]**.

Thank you for being a part of our literary journey, and we look forward to reading your review!

## WARM REGARDS

www.ingramcontent.com/pod-product-compliance
Lightning Source LLC
Chambersburg PA
CBHW071056290526
45795CB00004B/1520